To Pauline,

Don't trust everything you see!

even salt looks like sugar!!

Enjoy.

PArcHBlAke

June 2023

Penny Ann Lonsdale

authorHOUSE®

AuthorHouse™ UK
1663 Liberty Drive
Bloomington, IN 47403 USA
www.authorhouse.co.uk
Phone: 0800.197.4150

Published by AuthorHouse 06/17/2016

ISBN: 978-1-5246-3594-7 (sc)
ISBN: 978-1-5246-3595-4 (hc)
ISBN: 978-1-5246-3602-9 (e)

"Look not at the flask;
But at what it contains."

Part One

—From Riches to Rags!

I start with my maternal Great Grandmother from St. Lucia in the West Indies. Her name was Emelie; Emma for short, Emelie Mendez. The surname is Spanish; although her husband was white and from British Guyana. We believe a plantation owner who came to St. Lucia to look for more land or women.

He took Emma back to his hometown where they married and had their only daughter Harriet. But it wasn't long before Emma returned to St. Lucia as her husband turned out to be a womaniser as well as a good drinker who would occasionally raise his hand to her.

Her husband never returned to St. Lucia but would send money home to his wife.

Emma was very well off now and didn't want for anything; except her husband, but the man she married was not the one he became.

They only had one daughter (my Grandmother) named Phyllis who too had a good life with servants; piano lessons and private education in her early years. But dear Emma would be bored; bored, fed up and lonely and so would cook meals for families in the village who were less fortunate than her.

Her husband would send barrels filled with flour, oil, sugar, rice, spices whatever he thought she would need; all except himself.

We think she missed him terribly; my Gran was young and didn't know him that well so was used to life without a father.

The meals to the neighbours became plentiful to them but Emma would get very carried away and make far too many. At times she would leave cooked meals outside of her house for people to take; but they didn't take the food which would end up being left outside for days and days. In the end, folk would simply refuse her food altogether as they were not sure if it was freshly cooked or had been left outside. Emma would get terribly upset so they would just take it and not eat it so as not to offend.

Poor Emma would get very confused and think people were stealing from her when really, she had given so much away she had not kept track of things. She would accuse everyone, shouting out at passers by, knocking on doors for the return of money she thought she had lent; it got so bad that she was eventually admitted to the local mental hospital. We now realise that she either had a nervous breakdown or was showing early signs of Alzheimer's.

My Gran was taken away from her in the end. Things had to be sold to pay for the hospital fees and the family looking after my Gran would demand more money. Emma's husband had died out there in British Guyana unexpectedly, through drink and didn't leave any money. All money was lost due to gambling and womanising no doubt. Making money became scarce no one trusted him. He lost friends, family and money and died alone.

Anyway; my Gran was bought up by relatives who were not so well off; poor in fact, ending up with Harriet having to attend the local government school and being stripped of all of her luxuries. Life was pretty grim and different for her from now.

Then there was my grandfather; Ethelbert Devaux (French ancestors this time).

Now my Grandfather came from a family of HeadMasters; School Governors; Teachers, Professors and carpenters and so would fit in very well with Harriet's early life.

However young Harriet as a teenager got into the wrong crowd and ended up having a child while she was quite young and out of wedlock which was terribly frowned upon in those days. Then not long after giving birth, another child! All of this before she met my Grandfather.

But my grandfather took a strong liking to her for some reason and agreed to marry her and take on her two young sons as though they were his own until life began to take some further twists....

3

PART TWO

New Pastures and Greener Grass

So there is Ethelbert Devaux and Harriet Mendez agreeing to marry and start a new life together. Ethelbert is happy to take on Harriet's young babies as his own.

But doesn't want to stay and set up home in St. Lucia; he wants a new life in St. Vincent.

So the plan is for them to go to St. Vincent where he is to find work and a home and then get married so they can begin their lives.

That was the plan; but as my Mum would always say "What man plans; God wipes out".

Harriet became pregnant again but this time with Ethelbert's child and couldn't go to St. Vincent. So the new plan was for Ethelbert to go to find work, land to build their home on, send for Harriet and the children so a new life overseas could be started. Although plans had changed but at least Harriet still had a chance to settle in another island and begin a fresh life.

But this was a complete shame for Ethelbert's parents and he himself was utterly embarrassed deep down. Coming from an educated family, this was not what his parents had lined up for him. A young women with two very young children; both from different fathers who they never saw and now another child on they way! What was he thinking?

A very popular woman with the local men was Harriet by now and was much more experienced than Ethelbert. It was more likely that Harriet

had enticed Ethelbert and he was probably teased by his friends. Teased by his friends for his choice of a future wife but reprimanded severely by his parents for getting involved with such a woman.

So even if the trip to St. Vincent was a pie in the sky idea; it became reality and a way out for Ethelbert.

So Ethelbert leaves St. Lucia to start his adventure and with all good intention of keeping to the plans.

There were rumours of how he really loved Harriet and she loved him; but in her own way I guess.

They do say that the little girl who craves the love of her father will always be seeking love from different men while she looks for love, comfort and security and how they get confused with understanding the difference between sex and love. I came to realise just how true that saying actually was!

Ethelbert would always write letters and send money for Harriet but sadly Harriet would have other ideas.

She would be out partying as she thought she was missing out on life. Partying whenever and wherever she could. If there were parties three nights in a row; Harriet would be at all three.

I suppose she missed her own mother and her life of luxuries. When the money was gone, the family who looked after her failed to continue to care for her the way they used to. She wasn't best pleased living with poor relations so she rebelled.

Phyllis was born on 9th December 1936 and was named Phyllis Mendez (Harriet is not married remember so the children will always take the mothers family name-remember I said this!).

So Harriet was now a young woman with three very young children of her own. How on earth would she cope? Well she couldn't.

The child she had just before Phyllis were twin boys, but while in the hospital the nurses knew she couldn't cope and so smothered one of them with a pillow to end his young life allowing Harriet with the ability to now "cope."

Later on Harriet would be known for roaming the streets at night looking for her baby and shouting out "Mummy's coming for you, don't cry!".

We never got to work out exactly how old Harriet was when she had the children but we knew she was young.

Ethelbert was now in St. Vincent, had found work in an oil company. Oil is one of the largest manufactories in St. Vincent so finding work in that line was pretty easy.

It took quite sometime for Ethelbert to put a bit of money away to travel back to St. Lucia to see his baby daughter, but now there were rumours going around that Harriet was involved with yet another man; and pregnant again.

Ethelbert was truly embarrassed and ashamed with all of this and thought to never set foot in his birth land again.

His parents advised him that it was best to stay where he was and begin his new life out there. But curiosity got the better of Ethelbert and he had to see for himself exactly what was going on and hear the truth directly from Harriet's own mouth.

He visited Harriet in the old shack where she lived in Laborie. Ethelbert was dressed in smart pants and a crisp white shirt carrying gifts for his daughter and Harriet's boys. He was really hoping for the rumours to be lies about Harriet being pregnant again.

Harriet came to the door with one child on her hip and the other crying with a runny nose holding on to her ankles. He could see her stomach still swollen as the child's leg lay across it. When the child saw Ethelbert, he quickly smiled and turned to bury his head in Harriet's shoulder.

"So is it true then Harriet; that your pregnant again?" "Yes" Harriet replied with her head looking away.

They were not rumours about Harriet expecting again; it was the truth; he heard it for himself now.

"Ethelbert; you don't understand what it's like for me here. You took off to St. Vincent without us. You should have taken me with you. I was lonely; I missed you" was all that Harriet could say in her defence.

"You missed me so you went to the arms of another man? Where is this man now? Is he going to take care of you, make an honest woman of you like I was? Where is he Harriet? Where is this man and more to the point, who is he, what's his name?"

Harriet couldn't answer as she didn't 'know' the answer to his questions.

Harriet shifted the baby from her right to her left hip. The baby at her ankles wiped his nose on her skirt but Harriet didn't seem at all bothered. The child was without a nappy; a bare bottom and the one in her arms was with a full one. As she put the child down to rub her back you could see the full nappy hanging down low from his waist. The vest he had on was way too small. It was clear that Harriet was struggling.

"Can I see my daughter?" He asked as he stepped into the untidy house. Ethelbert followed Harriet into a small room with a big bed pushed up against the wall. On the bed were two pillows either side of the baby; his baby. No cot or no crib for her. "Where do the little boys sleep Harriet?" Ethelbert asked looking around for more space.

"Here with me in the bed" she said patting the bed gently so as not to wake Phyllis.

Ethelbert was shocked by this. A new father he may be; but he also knew that a mother sleeping in one bed with two toddlers and a baby was not right.

He looked down at Phyllis and moved her hand so he could see her face; he daren't wake her. She looked clean and content while sleeping. He gave Harriet the bag he brought; good thing he bought items of clothing for the boys as they surely needed new clothes.

Well you can imagine the hurt and the embarrassment Ethelbert now felt. He took out his wallet from his back pocket and handed Phyllis $10. "Buy some things for the children and look after yourself. I'll send more money for the baby". Harriet took the money and thanked him.

"I'll take the baby to your parents' house so they can see her" Harriet told Ethelbert as he left. "I'll send the money there so you can collect it while bringing the baby to them" Harriet realised now that she would have to keep to her word.

He had kept in touch with the occasional letter and sent money for Harriet but what she did with it was anyone's guess. Reports would go back to Ethelbert telling him that the baby wasn't clean when she visited and how it was always crying.

Ethelbert was hurt and confused now and felt he could never trust a woman again.

It was decided that arrangements were to be made for Ethelbert's parents to raise Phyllis as it was quite clear that Harriet was not fit to look

after so many young children especially with another one on the way; she just couldn't cope.

That was the last time Ethelbert visited St. Lucia.

PART THREE

-God Bless the Children-

So Ethelbert went back to St. Vincent where he stayed and never visited St. Lucia again; not even once! That was it for him; badly bruised and embarrassed he never returned.

His parents were looking after his daughter and so he would often receive reports about Phyllis together with photographs sent to update him on her life.

Thunderous skies strike the Devaux's again. Ethelbert took sick quite badly in St. Vincent.

He was in hospital where a kind local lady nursed him back to good health.

Common sense told Ethelbert that this lady was honest, true and from good stock as it were; which was just as well; his previous love didn't turn out quite the way he expected!

Eventually Ethelbert married this kind lady and went on to have nine children with her; (not in any particular order) Andrea - worked for the same oil company as Ethelbert; married and had three children.

Shirley - became a school teacher; her husband was killed in a car crash shortly after she gave birth to her only son, Nicolas. Shirley died from MS some years later on.

Ronald- A Mounted Policeman married and divorced an Asian lady. Not sure if he had children.

Henderson – worked in Forensic. Married but not sure on the amount of children.

Mandy- never married; no children but looked after her nieces and nephews during the day as an income.

Robert - became heavily involved in Politics; no children. He later died.

Rhonda - never married nor had children and just stayed at home keeping house. Died later.

Diane- worked her way up to became manager of the local post office. Never married neither had any children.

Helen - became a teacher and married a teacher who worked with special needs children; they had three children, emigrated to America. Helen later died; also from MS.

So many patterns!

But..... That was life in St. Vincent; for now.

There were photos around his new home of Phyllis; his daughter.

When his children were of age they would ask who the little girl in the photo was. "That's your cousin back in St. Lucia" he would say.

Oh dear; too embarrassed to even tell his children that they had an older sister and that she was born out of wedlock.

So there was Phyllis being raised by her paternal grandparents in a place called Caneries in St. Lucia from the tender age of just six months old.

Life was good for her, she was loved mainly by her grandfather Jackson and his younger sister Hyacinth who never married.

Obviously compensating for the parents who weren't around to raise her.

My mum would tell us that he had been a headmaster at a boys private school and would often teach her at home after school when she was of age.

He would also read and write letters for locals who were illiterate. He would make and repair household goods, even shoes.

Phyllis loved him dearly.

A majority of people from the West Indies had diabetes and heart problems due to the food that is high in starch and sugar.

The food is good nourishment and helps build bones, teeth and muscle.

This goes back to slavery days where black people would be out working in the field and doing heavy duty jobs like lifting, carrying and ploughing, so good solid food had to sustain them from the morning until nightfall when they would have their next and final meal.

Food had to be rich and filling so it could last and keep up their strength for the day through working in the hot sun.

My mum never mentioned anyone working on the fields or plantations so I guess our family missed these dreaded slavery times back in St. Lucia...

Jackson Devaux had diabetes and had to have his leg amputated from the knee down.

My mum would often say that he complained about his leg hurting long after the operation due to phantom pains.

Life became rather dark and dismal for him with only one leg. He wasn't able to get about as much and would have the odd fall now and again making him so irritable and frustrated. Although he made his own crutches he still felt restrained and held back; but still locals would come and visit him all the same and ask for favours. He would say he wasn't feeling up to it or to come back another day; knowing another day wouldn't make any difference. He clearly wasn't himself.

One afternoon as Phyllis skipped home from school some of the local children had shouted out that her grandfather had died.

I remember her saying that she had always thought they were referring to someone else...until she got home and she realised that her Dearest Grandfather had indeed passed away.

"Oh how I cried"; Phyllis would say. I could feel her pain as she said those words; the only father figure in her life had gone and so had the light!

PART FOUR

-Education; Education; Education-

Jackson Devaux and his wife had the following children. Ethelbert. Had Phyllis and 9 others.

Penelope married Claude and had Leroy (now a top brain surgeon in Washington)

Victoria (worked in Customs and now suffering from; guess what; MS!)

Phillip who had problems in the Army and had to leave.

Theodore was a Head master of the local school had daughters Dora, Liz, Phoebe and sons Charles and Peter.

Marcus was a pharmacists and had Sally who went from being a teacher to Head Mistress of the school that she attended as a child and two sons Simon and Jonathan.

Christopher died at a young age.

Now that her Grandfather had passed Phyllis was raised by her gran-aunt Hyacinth, who again she loved dearly. Things seemed to work so well with them. Hyacinth didn't have any children and Phyllis's parents were: well we know where they were!!

Phyllis was settled with home, family and life. Things were good and content for her at last; but for how long?

Some of her cousins were nearby who would attend the same school and visit each others houses so life was filled with fun and laughter.

But then Hyacinth was in and out of hospital with high blood pressure and diabetes. The family decided it was best for Phyllis to be in Gros Islet; a beautiful part of St. Lucia with her Uncle Theodore and his family until Hyacinth was home for good. Of course Phyllis would have preferred for her Aunt not to be in hospital but was happy to be with her cousins.

They all went to school together, Church, Bible studies, the market you name it; they was always together.

Church played a massive part in the lives of black families. It was where they felt safe, comfortable, had a lot in common with each other and where they could praise their one believer.

When things were not going right for them; when they felt all was lost they would take to Churches and the Bible.

I read somewhere that an old American woman who could not read; would easily recite the bible chapter and verse, but yet could not read a single word.

Church was where they would congregate and sing their hearts out and listen to the word of God; their God. When there was no money for food; When food was scarce; When times were hard; they never gave up.

They had God; they would pray together at home, in the Church and when things went right; it was down to God because God was all they had.

Phyllis loved Sunday School and really enjoyed the Bible stories. Sunday was the day when everyone would wear their best clothes, do their hair and look their smartest to attend the local Church. Even the poorest family with children going to school without shoes would have their best clothes put aside for Sunday service. You were never able to tell who was richer or poorer!

Then Dear Aunt Hyacinth passed away due to high blood pressure and diabetes.

Another sad time for Phyllis who was not even ten at the time.

Death did not leave her feeling settled at all. Who would care for her now?

Imagine a young girl never having anyone to call Mum or Dad? I've heard of either parent not being around; but not both. What a tragic life for one so young.

After Hyacinth's funeral they all decided it was best for Phyllis to go to Dennery and live with her Aunt Penelope and her husband Claude Martin

Penelope was one of Phyllis's grandfathers daughters. But good old Uncle Theodore was against that and suggested Phyllis live with him and his family in Gros Islet. He was the Headmaster at the local school and his two eldest sons Charles and Peter taught there as teachers.

It was one big happy family and Phyllis would soon settle after the death of her Aunt Hyacinth. Although nights were the worst time when she would cry herself to sleep thinking about her Grandfather and Aunt Hyacinth; oh how she missed them.

She would attend Gros Islet school. Even though children were not allowed to have any say in such matters she was so glad that her Uncle Theodore made such a suggestion to live with him and his family as she didn't know anyone in Dennery, so how could she live there? Honestly!!

PART FIVE

-Another One Bites the Dust-

Just when Phyllis was settled with moving on with her next family; tragedy takes place again. Thunder roars as tornados twist their ugly heads through the skies.

It wouldn't be long before Phyllis's Uncle Theodore would have to give up work due to illness. Then not long after that; he became worse and sadly died. Diabetes is wiping this family out one by one; well it seemed that way to Phyllis.

Theodore's oldest sons who taught in the local schools would now follow in their fathers footsteps and continue teaching there.

After the funeral of her Uncle Theodore, his sister Penelope who was previously in Aruba with her husband, decided that Phyllis was to move to Dennery. Her husband Claude Martin (not a nice man) was working in Aruba at the time.

Aruba had a large oil industry like St. Lucia and many folk would work there and send parcels and money back to their families.

Claude Martin didn't like the Devaux's as they were intelligent and lived comfortable lives; unlike his family who were poor and uneducated.

It was said how wicked he were to his wife Penelope, previously Devaux and would boss her around and shout at her in front of anyone who was there.

Things had to be his way because he was the man of the house; the only status he could claim I suppose.

Phyllis did not want to live with this side of her family; but who was she to argue with and where else could she go? The rest of the family seemed to be dying anyway; who was left?

Left to die next or left to be passed on to? It meant the same thing in Phyllis's eyes!

Dennery is an island mainly used for fishing and the cultivation of lime beans so not an exciting place for a young girl to grow up not really knowing her family there.

Dennery was and probably still is rather primitive in comparison to the other islands in the West Indies; rather backward if anything; where most people would have to go to the nearest island for produce if they didn't grow their own.

Cows, goats, pigs and sheep would be grazing on dry patchy grass; while hens and chickens would peck in pens at scraps.

Water had to be bought from the government system far away and many children would be bare footed.

Phyllis never liked it and always said it was dry land and you had to work hard to survive there. Oh she was not wrong.

So Phyllis headed off to a place that she had never been to before; to stay with people who she hardly knew.

Laughter stopped for Phyllis....

Aunt Penelope had her oldest son Leroy at the fee paying boys school, Victoria was at the girls convent while Aunt Penelope was with-child carrying Phillip her youngest.

Her husband Claude was in Aruba working as a carpenter.

Sad to say but the darker in skin colour; the more one would be frowned upon and seen as not pretty or not as attractive as the fairer one. A bit like blonde versus ginger I suppose. This was the bain of pretty much every child with darker skins life.

This stemmed from the slavery days when the darker folk would be out in the field and the fairer ones would be in the house working.

This was not just in St. Lucia, but in every black culture; Africans too. It's very old fashioned but it is still recognised and was frowned upon for a very long time until the black media would promote it by putting pictures in magazines and news papers of the darker race where it would be fully embraced and accepted more.

Phyllis was of very fair complexion; very slim, soft silky long hair and very pretty.

Aunt Penelope's children were darker in complexion and Victoria was a little chubby! But Victoria attended the Convent School for girls and Phyllis would have to attend the local school; Mount Pleasant Government School in fact. Victoria and Phyllis; Rivals from the start!

Poor Phyllis; first thing in the morning while the dew was still damp and fresh on the dry grass, she would have to take the animals out onto the field, clean the pigs sty, sweep the goat and sheep pen, put out their food, fetch their water amongst other things; all the donkey work really.

Goats, sheep, pigs and cows would then be left to graze on the dry grass.

Phyllis would be bare footed at times. Although she had a pair of shoes for Sunday school.

After that she would have to prepare and cook dinner; which would consist of chicken, or meat, with vegetables, dumplings etc etc.

No problem you may say; but the chicken had to be killed and plucked, gutted, washed and seasoned with salt, pepper, onions, garlic, ginger and spices before stewing or roasting. Even the spices had to be peeled and prepared. Vegetables would have to be boiled, dumplings would be made from scratch with white flour and corn meal; all by Phyllis.

After school it would be washing clothes by hand; as no washing machines were around at that time; ironing would be a flat iron resting on the stove until it got hot. Then there was the cleaning and the washing up, drying and putting away; all by poor little, skinny Phyllis.

All when chubby Victoria would be out playing with the boys and girls and making excuses not to do any domestic chores.

Phyllis would have to wear hand-me-downs. Claude would send gifts from Aruba for his wife and children; but nothing for Phyllis.

At times she could hear them munching on the nice cookies that had been sent from Aruba after Phyllis had gone to bed.

People from the other houses would see she was not treated fairly and would ask why poor Phyllis would be working like a donkey while Victoria would be playing in the fields. Penelope: her mother would say "Victoria has a stomach ache or a headache or homework"; spoiling her little Princess by making excuses that not even she would believe.

Victoria would make every excuse under the sun to prevent herself from lifting a finger to do any of the domestic chores. She would even prick her finger with a sewing needle to get out of doing the washing up. Anything to avoid hard work of mending and darning.

When Claude had returned from Aruba he would shout out to little skinny Phyllis "where's the food; I'm hungry!" If the meal were not on the table.

Breakfast was almost as plentiful as the dinner and Phyllis would have to be the one to prepare it while Princess Victoria was still in bed asleep!!

There were times when Victoria would sneakily place her dirty clothes in a pile with Phyllis's; hoping she would wash them.

When Phyllis refused; Aunt Penelope would tell her off for putting it there calling her own daughter lazy.

Not a nice way to be treated by any means. Phyllis was often teased for not knowing or for not having her father around.

How she coped and got through all of this no one knows; but she did; she got through it; eventually!!

School, Church, God, Prayers and Sunday school helped get her through it all.

That was where she felt comfortable and at ease with a break from the daily chores. The place where she found inner peace with her bible and note pad. Phyllis loved school, she loved learning.

But as soon as she hit puberty; she was taken out of school by her Aunt. We think for fear of her getting involved with boys and becoming pregnant, because let's face it; they didn't really want to take care of Phyllis let alone a baby of hers!

This did not please Phyllis who came from a background of scholars; how could they break such an important link with her?

Church would be the place where everyone would look their best in their smart clothes, hair styled to perfection with matching hats or ribbons.

Boys would give the girls the eye and tease them in school the next day; tease to later court no doubt!!

PART SIX

Follow Your Passion

One very wet and rainy morning; Phyllis took sick. All of this early morning fetching and carrying and being up with the early morning dew brought on a terrible illness for her.

She became very unwell with a high temperature and dizzy spells together with awful aches and pains in her knees.

She could barely walk, let alone prepare breakfast for the household; which had to be done before school.

Phyllis came home from the fields in tears and in pain limping from both legs and holding on to anything she could use to stabilise herself with.

She was sent to bed by her Aunt and told to rest for the day? Phyllis could still hear the orders for food being shouted out by her Uncle.

Her Aunt Penelope was under the impression that Phyllis was shying away from work and so sent her out the next day. Not so as Phyllis had to cut that task very short by making her way home early.

On her return she had seen a friend of her Aunt Penelope's; Bernice Long who was on her way to see her local doctor.

Miss Bernice could clearly see that Phyllis was looking very sickly and unwell. She told Penelope that she would take Phyllis with her to the doctors.

Penelope seemed to care more about Phyllis having to leave the animals in the field without knowing who would fetch them back and obviously worrying that her husband Claude will cause quite a fuss with having his breakfast late.

In those days back in the West Indies having respect for your elders was a big thing and still is no doubt.

If you happened to see one of your parents' friends while out; you would address them as Miss or Mr followed by their Christian name.

If you saw someone who you knew was a teacher; they would be addressed as Sir or Teacher added to their Christian name; your cousin would be referred to as Cousin followed by the Christian name.

Even if you saw strangers at the bus stop you would automatically say "Good morning" or "Good night" and it still goes on to this day.

So Miss Bernice took Phyllis to the doctors with her. As soon as the Doctor saw her he could see she was unwell and said she had a very high fever and would need to be hospitalised. Examining her confirmed this instantly.

Miss Bernice would go back to Penelope for Phyllis's clothes then off to the hospital; Colony Hospital in Dennery to be precise.

But the hospital being as primitive as it were in those days didn't have the medication that was needed to treat Phyllis.

The doctor at the hospital apologised to Phyllis that she would have to go to another hospital for treatment. He was sorry for sending her there; thinking she wouldn't know anyone.

"I'm from Gros Islet Doctor; I'm not from here!" Phyllis would reply in a matter of fact voice.

The Doctor was surprised that anyone would want to leave Gros Islet for Dennery until Phyllis explained her journey to him.

Aunt Penelope and Uncle Claude were not happy with having to spend money to send Phyllis away; but needs must; she was in so much pain and agony that to keep her any longer would be cruel.

So back on the boat to her beloved Island Gros Islet; only to be hospitalised.

Not the greatest of reasons to be back in your own county!

Phyllis was diagnosed with rheumatoid arthritis and was in hospital for over four weeks. This worried Phyllis greatly as everyone who went into hospital never came out alive; this she experienced with her relatives so one could clearly understand her concerns.

In hospital and placed on a ward; Phyllis would sit up in bed when she wasn't sleeping and watch the nurses at work. She watched them care

for the patience, attend to them, wash them and administer their drugs. She saw how they were dressed in stiff white uniforms and soft shoes. The watch they wore on their upper chest looked so impressive to her and how the patience would depend on the nurses was marvellous; she liked that; she liked that very much.

Phyllis would have visits from her cousins after they had finished school. Her Aunts and Uncles; even her mother Harriet had visited.

Family would bring fruit, drinks, and books for Phyllis. Oh how she felt so special.

By this time; the amount of children Harriet had, grew; enormously; Conrad - a lovely brother- travelled to and from St. Lucia to London and sadly died.

Oscar-twin whose brother was suffocated by the nurse- would also travel to and from England.

Phyllis - Read On!

Godfrey- lived in America and died from being a heavy drinker. Doreen- lives in UK and travels back to St. Lucia.

Belinda- never left St. Lucia.

Elaine- never left St. Lucia Annabelle- Never left St. Lucia Louise- Never left St. Lucia Carol- Set up home in USA

Two other babies had died at childbirth; not sure where they fit.

Thirteen children; Just as well Ethelbert gave Phyllis to his parents to raise and left for a better life; nine to be exact!

It was later discovered that Harriet had never been herself again after her twin son had died. He was buried in a box behind her house and she would often go looking for him. Calling out "mummy's here; don't cry".

Then when Phyllis was taken away she was terribly saddened. Her first daughter taken from her arms. She would miss Phyllis so much and would speak of her constantly. Some of her other children would grow to dislike Phyllis because of this.

Before Phyllis was summoned to Dennery, She would often visit her mother who would plait her hair and put in pretty ribbons.

Oh how pretty she looked; Harriet would be proud; proud and sad all at the same time.

PART SEVEN

-Hired Help; No Pay-

With Phyllis out of hospital and taking things easy, she heads back to Gros Islet to be with her cousins as before.

Oh she was so happy not to be back in Dennery fetching and carrying like hired help without any pay.

As she got better she would attend after school classes at Gros Islet school where she would learn Handicraft; sewing, knitting, dress making and crocheting. This she loved; being with her family, attending school and most of all; not having to play maid. Oh Phyllis was happy once more.

She would often sit and wonder just how her deceased family would have felt if they knew she were taken out of school at such a young age. I can only imagine their devastation knowing how strongly education played such an important part in their lives.

Later after Phyllis had gained strength and was back on her feet again she was introduced to an older white couple who were Missionaries staying in St. Lucia.

Albert and Cynthia Large settled in a place called Mon Repos just passed a town named Micoud. They didn't have any children of their own.

Phyllis would attend to their domestic needs where she was actually paid.

She would cook her nice dishes for them; peas and dumpling soup, cornmeal porridge and her fabulous cakes and buns with minced fruit that had been soaked in red wine for many months. Phyllis would also dress Mrs Large after her bath.

Another couple of young girls; Petra and Wendy who were sisters would do the washing and the ironing for them.

As time went on Mr and Mrs. Large aged and so decided to go back to England. They were getting on in age and most of their friends had returned to England so they decided to follow suit.

Not long after Mr and Mrs Large had returned to England; Phyllis received a letter.

The letter was from England. From a gentleman by the name of Titus Roberts.

Titus was from Dennery and would attend the same Church and Sunday school as Phyllis when she was there. He remembered her and obviously did some homework to be able to write to her and ask for her hand in marriage.

Phyllis always worried that any time soon her Aunt Penelope would drop the bombshell on her and summoned her back to Dennery or that someone else would die causing her to go and live with yet another relative.

Phyllis wanted to avoid going back there and so decided to take up Titus's offer of marriage.

Her Uncle Marcus was in Aruba at the time and heard of this. He agreed to pay her fares for her to go to England, a few of her cousins had already left St. Lucia for London so for a short while Phyllis would stay with them in West London before she would leave to be married and live in Yorkshire!!

PART EIGHT.

Vacancies; but no rooms!

It's 1955 and Phyllis is 19 years old and about to leave St. Lucia; The Land of sea for England.

In my opinion every island has beautiful sunshine and beaches and it's only the accent that divides them. There are beautiful parts of each island along with run down areas and I'm sure if you were placed onto an island with your eyes closed; it would be very hard to work out where you were until you heard an accent.

Liz her cousin had bought Phyllis an autograph book and made arrangements for her close family and friends to write in it (have always loved that idea). This book was given to Phyllis before she boarded the ship that set sail for England.

Of course Phyllis was so happy to be going on to pastures new but sad to be leaving her home country.

Her Mother Harriet came to see her off; along with other family members. Oh there were tears; lots of them, especially from Harriet who she hugged so tightly and whispered to Phyllis; "Don't forget me; and please write to me daughter!"

Phoebe (sister to Liz and Dora daughters of Theodore) were already in England; London, Ealing to be precise, so Phyllis would spend some time with her before she travelled to Yorkshire to get married.

Phoebe and Phyllis got on really well so to be living together was a dream come true for them. Phoebe was born in February and Phyllis in

December of the same year so they were quite close in age. Oh how they would cry through laughter as they reminisced the past.

Travelling across, Phyllis would sail through many countries and end up in Southampton.

On the ship there were many people from other islands. How strange it must have been to be with so many people from different parts of the Caribbean, the same colour; yet only their accents to tell them apart.

I cannot imagine leaving a hot climate of family and friends to travel to a cold country where you hardly know anyone.

If you were lucky (and I mean lucky) to come over on a government scheme permit to work on the railways or the Post Office; the government would find dwellings for you; other than that you were left to find work and a home independently.

Housing was hard to find and with a lot of problems to match. Vacancies but no room -many signs in the window saying; (yes you guessed it)

No Dogs;

No Blacks;

No Irish.

Fancy seeing signs like that with your suitcases in hand in a country colder than your own; how welcoming!

If you were lucky you would get a room where you would not only share the kitchen and bathroom but you would only have two rings to the stove to use; milk would be kept in the cellar where it was cold and even jelly would set there!!

African families would settle in some areas and were able to buy houses with two rooms.

They would live in one room with their family and rent out the other. This was of great benefit for families from the Caribbean but it was not all the time that Africans and West Indians got along together.

Jamaicans started a thing called The Pardoner. Word and mouth would get around where a head person (and this could be anyone who announces it) would be given £5 or £10 each week from each person in the group. A group could be anything up to twenty people. When the money was paid by everyone; it was rolled up in a band and given to whoever was next in line to receive it. Then it would start again, then the week after the

next person in line would get the money and so on. I suppose it was like a pyramid come lottery.

There were never any problems; people would know whose group they were in; when to pay the money and how much. It was always paid on time; every Friday.

This was the only way people could save and buy big things like furniture and deposits for houses as credit or loans were not given to them.

When the houses were bought they were able to rent out rooms to other folk from other West Indian islands. What a pleasure it must have been to see signs saying "Vacancies" and it be true to its word.

Then the struggle was with the food and the cosmetics and hair products that were different; where would they be purchased from? They would have to travel to places like Shepherds Bush, Brixton and Harlesden to get simple things such as rice and dried lentils until yams, green bananas, plantain and other provisions were imported.

Trying to get the correct shade of tights was such a problem for black woman. With women being different shades the whole idea was being able to wear tights so close to their natural skin colour that people wouldn't think you had any on. But in England you could only buy black and white and American tan which was supposedly for the women of colour; but one colour did not suit all and some would just look ridiculous with dark skin and light colour tights; but what other choice did they have? It was American tan or bare legs and in the much colder climate the former would win!!

Let's not forget the hairdressers; well, there weren't any for black people. Men would have to visit a friend who had a steady hand and a chair as well as a pair of scissors.

Woman would have to do the same and visit a friend; only they would take a hell of a lot longer and need a lot more accessories!

They needed rollers; wash basins, combs, brushes, hair oil, styling lotion, towels and a hair dryer. To style the hair they would have to use an iron comb which would be placed on the fire to get hot, this would then be used to comb the hair to give it a straight look. So you can see why it took so long; a lot of grooming and pampering was needed for this as Afro hair is not straight; but it was worth it!

Now of course after a long week at work or trying to find work left them feeling so exhausted they would obviously need an outlet. They were not welcomed in pubs; so that was ruled out and they could forget dance halls and let's be honest here; the taste in music was somewhat very different.

So whoever owned the house or had the kindest Landlord; that's where the party was held.

Parties would last all night from Saturday night until the early hours of Sunday morning.

Food, company, drinks and music was all they needed for them to feel at home then. (no different from pubs really) It wasn't until a little while after where they would start to charge an entrance fee to cater for the food and drink.

Then they would start to hire out halls of residents and then every Saturday night they would dress up in their best frocks and dance the night away.

PART NINE

Plastering over the Cracks.

Before we visit Phyllis in her new town; let's take a look at what she left behind.

As you know Phyllis's mother Harriet went on to have more children. It became common knowledge that one of her daughters was swapped in the hospital just after birth.

When Harriet had her daughter lying in the hospital cot a mother in the next bed had swapped her with her own child. We are led to belief that the woman's child was dark and would not fit in with her home life (shade wise) all Harriet's children were of the fairer shade and it looks as though this lady's husband was also fair. However not the same shade as the man who impregnated her, for he was of the darker shade. So it made sense for her to swap the babies.

Harriet loved children and raised Belinda as her own even knowing full well of what went on. But having so many children it wouldn't matter to her for Belinda's father was not around anyway.

To bring money into the home Harriet would take bundles of neighbours' clothes down to the river to wash. This she could do with the children around her where she could keep an eye on them; well the ones she had left! Another one of her daughters was not raised by her. Doreen was brought up by someone else as there were just too many for Harriet to look after.

Ironing she refused to do as that would have to be done inside and Harriet didn't like to keep the children in; so washing clothes by the river was where she made her money.

Back in Dennery where Titus senior was married to Jennifer Roberts they had eight children. Titus Roberts Snr was a Minister in the Bocage Gospel Hall Church in Dennery. This Church was where Phyllis would attend when she had lived there.

Titus Snr and Jennifer had the following children; (not in this order)

Titus -AKA Junior

Gideon - The nice one!

Hilton - Married a white lady named Jean

Lynne Roberts

Tracey

Elouise

Jeremy

Cammy

There was another branch to the Church in Dennery where Mr Large was the Minister. It worked out that the marriage between Titus and Phyllis was of an arranged one; possibly between the two ministers.

Titus (Junior) was from a good family as his father was a minister and Phyllis was from a God fearing honest family so it seemed only right that they were perfectly matched; or were they?

Phyllis when she was in St. Lucia would dress Mrs Large as she suffered from bad and painful arthritis. Phyllis would dry her after she took a bath, sprinkle scented powder on her toes and crevasses and dress her.

Junior's mother had three brothers; George who was a teacher; Wallace and Francis who ended up working in Aruba.

Junior who cooked so well would go to his Uncle George's house and cook food and make cakes and bread and other delights. A strange set up to have your son cook for your brother, especially when you have daughters; but hey!

But hey indeed; it was later discovered that George would Interfere sexually with Junior. We have a strong feeling that the family knew this which was why Junior was shipped off to England.

That is what they did in those days; there was no social services or children's Homes so it was up to the family to do the right thing by the

child (and the family name) so as not to bring shame onto the family; plastering over the cracks instead of tackling the main issue.

So it was agreed that Junior and Phyllis would marry. Phyllis had finally travelled to Yorkshire; Huddersfield where she would become Mrs Roberts and begin her new life.

PART TEN

It's off to work we go

Life in London with her cousins was great when they were all together; before they married and settled.

Dora, Phoebe's younger sister came over to the UK from St. Lucia where she worked for the Civil Service as a clerical assistant in the local Post Office Treasury.

Soon after arriving in England she found a job in Oxford Street working in Tate and Lyle Tea Shop making breakfast and lunches.

Dora of course wanted to work within the civil service again but every post she went for she was declined. They would refuse her application or not even see her for an interview. She was "not qualified for this type of work" were their words.

So Tate and Lyle it was. White collar worker roles were for whites. The gentlemen would have jobs in banking, newspapers or insurance and the women would be typist, receptionist or clerks and they would all be white. But no English person would ever want to work in a tea shop so these were the only jobs that were available for people of colour.

One of Dora's uncles was a teacher back in the West Indies and of course wanted to carry on teaching. But could he get a teaching job? Oh no; he was told "the children would not understand him".

Joseph Jacobs speaks perfect English to this day; so instead went into the Post Office and worked his way up the ladder to area manager. He could never let go of teaching and would teach his children and others youngsters who were struggling in class.

Dora was very busy and her role was hard working. She would have to take orders, make the dishes, serve and take the money and that was just during the day. After the shop was closed the tables had to be wiped; chairs turned over on top of the tables and floors mopped. I'm hoping there was staff employed to do the washing up!

Dora, along with Phyllis, Phoebe and Victoria spoke very good English with hardly any accent detected; Dora remembers a group of young white lads coming in for breakfast and hearing Dora speak asked; "Where did you learn to speak like that?".

They were quite impressed and left a hefty tip for her.

PART ELEVEN

-What's yours is mine-

So Phyllis leaves London and heads for Huddersfield to meet Titus Junior.

Her cousins were there to see her off at Paddington Station where she would board the train to Huddersfield.

There he was at the station waiting for her with his two brothers. Poor Phyllis, she wasn't quite sure what Junior looked like. Of course she had seen him in Church but that was some time ago back in Dennery. When Junior left, she didn't see him off; didn't even know he had left until she got a letter from him. It was a good thing he knew who he was meeting otherwise this greeting would have been a touch embarrassing.

Luckily his brothers were there to help break the ice and make a fuss of her as Junior was, shall we say not too forth coming with greeting Phyllis.

They had no where to live at the beginning so Phyllis would live with his brother Jeremy and his wife Matilda and Junior with his brother Gideon; only until they were married.

Just when Phyllis thought she had left unpleasant times back in Dennery; they seemed to have followed her all the way to the UK.

There was no home for her and now had to live with her brother-in-law to be.

There was no wedding dress for her; this had to be borrowed from one of the sister in laws; which ended up being too big with not enough time to have it altered; and to add to more woes; none of her family members attended the wedding.

Not long after the wedding they were able to get a council house; the top floor to a two bedroom maisonette on Adelaide Road.

His family suggested Phyllis try the local factory for work! Factory! Phyllis!

Good Luck with that! Phyllis knew she was not raised to work in such a place and wanted to do training in Saint Elizabeth West; the local hospital.

A nurse was what she wanted to be; but being black and from the West Indies Phyllis would only be trained as far as an SEN (State Enrolled Nurse) rather than an SRN (State Registered Nurse) but before that she could only be an auxiliary, but hey; that would do nicely; for now.

From the time Phyllis was in hospital as a young child and saw the care and respect the nurses gave and received; Phyllis knew from that moment on she wanted to be a nurse.

Instead of having to fetch and carry and being made a fool of by her cousin Victoria and her parents; Phyllis wanted to have a purpose and make a difference somewhere and to someone.

She enjoyed working for the Larges when she was in St. Lucia, they loved her cooking and appreciated her good will. Phyllis wanted that gratuitous feeling again and she knew she could never obtain this from working in a factory.

That was the beginning of their problems. From the moment Phyllis came home to let Junior know that she were to begin her training; Junior felt demoralised. His face dropped while his nostrils flared knowing his wife was looking for a career which would mean prospects, chances and great advantages for her, but a dead end job at the said factory for him.

Married life for Phyllis was not what she had hoped for; it was not how she saw the marriages of her family members back in St. Lucia. Phyllis was expecting this "arranged married" to be a partnership where love would grow between them; ideas shared and plans be made together but how far from her expectations was she? Very far; very far indeed. This was a marriage of convenience; but for who?

Phyllis begun her training at Saint Elizabeth West Hospital; Huddersfield. Oh how the matron loved her.

Working at the hospital was an escape from life at home as home was clearly not how she expected it.

Junior would spend time with his brother Jeremy and his wife while Phyllis would be at home tidying, cooking and keeping house when she wasn't at work. Her spare time would be taken up with revising, sewing and reading the Bible; even if Junior were home or not.

Jeremy's wife Matilda was not nice at all: she envied Phyllis very much. She felt that Phyllis was punching above her weight being with her brother in law and not working in the factory with the rest of them. Matilda felt as though Phyllis were looking down on her; not so; Matilda was just being her jealous self.

And we know why; all of the Roberts men were very fair in skin colour while all the women were very dark. Phyllis was very fair and liked by the brothers; this did not sit very well with Matilda at all.

She would take full advantage of Phyllis and Junior would not say a single word. He knew it irritated Phyllis and would feel smug with seeing her upset and look on with delight.

Matilda would visit and help herself in their kitchen to rice, butter, flour etc etc and just say "Titus; I'm taking this" or "Junior; I'll take that" without any regard for Phyllis or how it got there.

The ladies in the house downstairs would call Phyllis stupid for allowing this to happen. But Phyllis was very soft and timid and without her family on her side; she felt very alone and isolated and would never dare retaliate in voice nor action.

Phyllis was rather skinny; another reason for Matilda to become green with envy; so skinny that Phyllis would go into the store for underwear and tell staff her bra size was 34B in order to purchase more. This was clearly not true as Phyllis had to fill AA size bras with tissues.

She would sew up the sides of the bra and stuff tissue into them for a better and more bulkier look.

As well as her attire; Phyllis would try to look more shapely and order tablets to increase her appetite and weight, but she had trouble swallowing them so she would crush them with the back of two spoons and add them to milk but this would just make her sick which defeated the object. In the end Phyllis would just stick to sewing the sides and filling the bras.

When Phyllis got paid Junior would take the money and hand enough back to her so she could do the shopping. When she returned home with

the shopping Junior would demand the till receipt and check everything single item off against the receipt. Whatever money was left he would ask her for the change.

Phyllis knew no better but still; in her heart of hearts: she knew it was not right.

- if you keep doing good, you can't go wrong -

At least they attended Church together; Junior and Phyllis. Well up until the wedding anyway. After that Phyllis would go by herself or meet her sister in Laws there.

Back home in St. Lucia it was the tradition to attend Church and once home the wives or females of the family would be in the kitchen cooking and on the table you would see a massive spread of;

Rice and Peas (kidney beans in fact; not peas) Macaroni Cheese

Roast Chicken or lamb, or beef

Roast potatoes

Vegetables would be orca, spinach, or even callalou

Roasted Breadfruit

Salad

Gravy

Imagine the washing up though; which was often done by the ladies so Phyllis would try to keep with tradition in Huddersfield, just maybe not so much food. To be honest; there were not that many dishes to put all the food in anyway!

One of Junior's good points out of the very few was that he was a really good cook and at times would prepare meals for him and his wife. Not very often though. He was also very clean and thorough around the home.

After the cooking and washing up the ironing and darning would be next so by the time you were ready to sit down it was almost time for bed. Would hate to think what time they would retire to bed if they had children? And don't forget there would usually only be two rings on the stove; the oven would be too small to hold everything at once so things would take an awful lot longer.

There were no steam irons either and Phyllis's uniform would need to be washed, starched hung out to dry and pressed by splashing water on them to make ironing easy. There was no spray starch or Easy Iron Spray in those days!

The hospital did provide a laundry service so nurses could hand in their uniforms to be washed and pressed before being returned but Phyllis would never hand hers in.

She would always want to do hers herself as she loved the thought of seeing her uniform pressed sharply and hanging up ready to wear. Phyllis took a lot of pride in her clothes; let's face it all her clothes were shop bought from new now and not handed down from the oldest relative as before.

Phyllis loved working in the hospital even though her role started on the geriatric ward, cleaning and fetching water for the patients. I suppose there was always a fear of getting fired, and bringing shame on the family back home, so there was a pleasing element in her work where she would never refuse to do anything. Plus Phyllis did not want to remain as an auxiliary an SEN was where she was heading so she felt by showing potential, she would be noticed and moved on quite soon.

So you can imagine Phyllis's delight but Junior's annoyance; if she told him that is. But she didn't tell him as she knew that would mean him taking more of her money. Her application was successful for her to begin training for her SEN role.

Phyllis felt it strange that the nurses on the ward would have time for idle chat when she were an auxiliary; but as soon as she began her training as a nurse they didn't have so much time and would hardly speak to her.

Phyllis would be hands on to do all the jobs regardless. The English nurses loved that as it meant less work for them.

They would all be in the staff room chatting, laughing, taking longer tea and lunch breaks arriving late for duty knowing Phyllis would be there to do their part.

Phyllis was always on time for her shifts; in fact she was always on time for everything. One of her ultimate bug bearers was being late. She despised people being late and hated waiting. She felt it rude and ignorant of them; "Leave with plenty of time" she would say.

There was one person who did like Phyllis very much and that was the Matron. When she would ask Phyllis where the other nurses were she would make excuses for them and say they were looking for items in the stock room or in the kitchen fetching something for the patients.

After Phyllis had run out of excuses and received no thanks from the nurses the Matron realised that her ward was not running quite like the clockwork she hoped for. She had caught the nurses sky larking and gave them a good telling off.

This did not sit kindly with them and so they would save the dirty jobs for Phyllis.

They would tell the patients that it was Phyllis's job to change and empty the bed pans and so every time a patient needed one they would call on Phyllis. Some of the patients would actually shout out loud "I don't want that darkie touching me" or "Anyone but that coloured Nurse" but when there were no other nurses around they had no choice but to sit and wait or apologise. Phyllis being Phyllis wouldn't wait for either and would tell them they'd have a long wait otherwise.

She would not only fetch the bed-pan, she would wash the patients, dry them, change their clothes and leave them sitting up smiling with neatly folded sheets spread around them. When Phyllis would fold back the curtains and present them to the rest of the ward the patients would be sitting up straight looking fresh and so pleased.

It wasn't too long before the patients were saying "Can I have the nice nurse please?" And refuse the English nurses.

When Phyllis had to change wards to continue her training the patients were very upset. One of the patients gave Phyllis a lovely gold necklace and thanked her for taking good care of her.

PART THIRTEEN

- Being With-Child-

As part of the training Phyllis was sent to work in the theatre to be a Theatre Nurse Assistant where she would have to set up the medical apparatus for the operations, check the equipment, ensure supplies were plentiful and all electrical equipment was in good working order. One of her duties was to count and weigh the cotton swabs that were used to soak up the blood during the operations.

Being an assistant didn't last too long as Phyllis kept on fainting. The smell of the blood caused nausea where she would have to be taken out of the theatre for air.

This happened once too often leaving the head surgeon most annoyed. Happy for the Matron though as Phyllis was back on the geriatric ward to attend to senior patients again.

But Phyllis still felt nauseous after returning and began to feel tired and drained during her shift.

There was a set rota for staff to start early; late or to split their shift. A split duty would start at 8am, finish at 12.30. Nurses would have to be back on the ward for 4pm and finish for the evening at 9pm.

But this continued and didn't seem to want to shift; Phyllis couldn't understand why until she visited the Dr who, after examining and asking questions confirmed she was pregnant.

She thinks Junior was pleased, but she could never tell. He asked when the baby was due and paid a little more attention by cooking the odd meal for her but that was about it because even that was short lived.

The Matron had seen how enthusiastic and interested in nursing Phyllis was so she had encouraged her to go further and set herself for the SEN (State Enrolled Nurse) exam.

Phyllis did and passed to become an SEN.

No point in telling Junior as he wasn't used to being joyous!

Meanwhile back at Adelaide Road; things were not anywhere near the happy times Phyllis had on the ward. You would have thought that being with-child would change the mood at home somewhat; but no, it most certainly didn't.

On the ward however; The patients loved her, the Matron respected her and even those nurses grew to like her. But to go home become a chore that she did not look forward to as she received none of the above from Junior.

Yorkshire was cold; very cold and the evenings would often start to get dark very early. With Junior taking her money it took quite some time to save up for a winter coat and a pair of boots. Phyllis's shoes had holes in the soles and she would end up having to wear her nurses shoes to work which was forbidden. You were not allowed to wear any part of your uniform outside of the hospital as this would bring germs onto the ward. This went for shoes as well. However the Matron could clearly see Phyllis's predicament and so she turned a blind eye to it.

A lot of the nurses' husbands or beaus would either meet them on the hospital grounds so they could walk home together or be met at the bus stop to be driven home.

Phyllis would just watch the couples walk on by or the nurses get into the cars of whoever they were courting and drive off.

Oh how Phyllis wished that Junior would one day meet her on the hospital grounds or at the bus stop. Not because she wanted him to but just because she longed for Junior to turn into a good companion for her; but to no avail; not even with her being with- child would he even think of doing something as nice.

Anyway Phyllis would be too scared to ask him for fear of his response.

At times she would get home quite late due to missing one bus and have to end up waiting even longer in the cold for the next one. She didn't mind missing the bus as it meant not seeing the loving couples; she just didn't like the waiting, especially in the cold.

When Phyllis would finally get home, she would be accused of meeting other men. She would try to explain but would be quietened down with a slap; even though she was with-child!

This was getting to become quite a habit now and there was a time when he picked up a rolling pin and threatened to hit her with it. Phyllis fainted right in front of him which really worried Junior.

The next thing Phyllis knew; Junior was sat beside her on the bed waving smelling salts under her nose to revive her.

After that short sharp shock Phyllis made sure she was on time for the first bus after her shift. This was difficult when the lonely patients on the ward would always want to talk to her; but needs must; she was on a mission to get home but still had to take things easy, being with-child.

PART FOURTEEN

- Only an Officer; Never a Gentleman-

Phyllis arrived home from work one afternoon only to see an official letter on the table addressed to Titus Roberts Junior. Dare she read it? was it left there for her to read on purpose?

There was no sign of Junior at home so Phyllis quickly but carefully opened the letter and left it, just as she found it before going to lie down. Junior was called up to do National Service. He was to be a Rifle Man.

Phyllis pretended not to see the letter just as she found it and went for a lie down.

A little while later Junior returned and told her that he would only be at home until the end of the week. He had received the letter quite some time ago but chose not to tell her. All of his family knew; Phyllis was the last to be told but yet felt elated with happiness at the thought of him not being around.

Phyllis had been secretly buying baby clothes and would have to leave them in her locker to save the Spanish Inquisition.

But oh this was such wonderful news for her; she could bring the clothes home, wash and iron them and have the house to herself. No more accusations, no more having to hide money. It was going to be pure bliss. And it was; until he came home when Phyllis was about to give birth.

They had a daughter; a beautiful baby girl they named Andrea Roberts. Born on 6th March 1959 at The Royal Maternity Home.

In those days the husband was not allowed to be in the delivery suit so Junior would be left to pace the floor outside until he was allowed to enter. By that time baby Andrea was cleaned up and in a blanket sleeping in Phyllis's arms.

Ten days was the length of time that Mothers would have stay in hospital after the birth unless they had a cesarean. That would give Junior enough time to sort things out at home; well his own things, as he would be getting ready to go back into the Army. He seemed to like it there and was always in some kind of a hurry to return.

Oh how Phyllis loved her daughter. She would sing to her, cradle her, pray with her, rock her to sleep, make sure she was always clean and smelling of cream and powder after her bath. Phyllis was organised and efficient and knew exactly what to do.

She didn't breast feed for long; she said it made her feel dizzy and light headed so after a few days Andrea was bottle fed.

Junior would feed Andrea but never change a nappy or hardly ever play with her. He would just look over the cot at her.

At night Phyllis would take a flask of hot water which she would keep by the bed with the milk in the bottle waiting for Andrea to wake during the night.

All nappies were terry ones as disposables were not yet around.

Phyllis would pride herself with having beautiful white nappies lined up on the line in the garden after having being soaked in Milton. The ladies downstairs would always comment on them being so white when they were left out on the line in the garden; there were times when they would take the washing in for her if it started raining.

Milton was used to soak the nappies in instead of throwing away the water after sterilising the bottles; this would make the nappies white.

Phyllis once left Junior with Andrea while she went to the shops; on her way up the stairs she could hear Junior shouting "Shut up; what are you crying for?" His voice bellowing down the stairs.

Phyllis burst into the room "Why are you shouting at her; she's only a baby" She roared back just like a lion would to protect its young.

This scared the life out of Phyllis as she couldn't believe her reaction towards Junior but at the same time she knew that it wouldn't be too long before a slap would be coming her way.

She couldn't chance it; she grabbed the baby from the crib and held her closely.

But no one shouts at Junior and gets away with it; a slap landed on her face; then another on the other side.

Phyllis was screaming and so was Andrea but for different reasons. Andrea was hungry while Phyllis was simply angry and what made it worse was having to shield her baby from its father.

The ladies from downstairs came running up banging on the door and shouting out "Why are you beating her? She's just a young girl; look at the size of you to her! Leave her alone". "She's just had a baby as well!"

With that Junior left for his brother's house pushing past the ladies who came in to comfort Phyllis and the baby from this awful ordeal. Phyllis in tears and shaking while being comforted by neighbours.

Junior was on special leave from the army but went back before he was due to return; Phyllis was delighted as she could play at being a happy mother once again. How can married life be better on your own? It was for Phyllis who got used to the fact that Junior would come and go when he pleased. She loved it when he left as she knew he wouldn't be back for quite sometime and that pleased Phyllis. It's when the days turned into weeks that worried her; as she would always know that anytime now he'd be back and anything would allow his temper to flare up.

PART FIFTEEN

Liars, cheats and thieves!

Up until the time Andrea was born, Phyllis was very lonely. She longed for the family life she had back in St. Lucia with her Grandfather and her Dear Aunt Hyacinth and her cousins.

She longed for that companionship she left behind in London that she had with her family there.

She almost felt cheated now; conned even, to know that the chance of any kind of relationship with Junior would never be and wasn't even on the cards to begin with.

He was hardly kind; nor loving to his wife, neither to his daughter for that matter. How could Phyllis ever be happy with such a person, such a man! She lived in total fear of him. She would jump whenever he raised his voice; and he may even not have been shouting! how could life ever be good?

She lived a life with no one to really confined in; no one to tell her inner most secrets to, as she'd be damned if she were to even think of keeping a diary.

On the same ward there was a young girl just like Phyllis. She was Irish and came from a family with older brothers.

Phyllis would talk to her as she too had a husband who she wasn't too fond of either.

They became great friends as they had so much in common but their shift patterns altered somewhat and they would go weeks without being able to speak to each other due to cross shifts.

While Phyllis was away from work having Andrea; she missed her friend. She missed the chats and hearing about the girls life and talking about her own!

In those days there was no such thing as maternity leave so when a women left work to have a baby she wasn't expected to come back. But Phyllis took three months off from work and returned once she found a suitable childminder for Andrea.

Junior would literally come and go as he pleased even though he were doing his National Service. He would come home and be out early the next day, stay away for days and then go straight back in the Army. He would come back home and be off again. But Phyllis started to notice strange things about him.

He would cook some food only enough for himself and lock away what was left in his wardrobe once he'd eaten so Phyllis couldn't get to it. He would also start to wash his own clothes. Phyllis thought this was strange but couldn't quite put her finger on the reason for his behaviour.

Phyllis would have to hide money under her side of the mattress as if it were left anywhere else, Junior would simply take it without asking.

It would be hidden in the wardrobe behind her clothes and he'd find it, to the back of the bread bin and he'd find it, in pots and again he would find it. A game to him no doubt as he must have felt victorious when he found it.

Unlike Phyllis who would be heart broken.

In the end she opened a Bank Account where she knew he could never get to it; well so she thought!

She had often gone to the Bank to withdraw money to pay the childminder and other things only to find that money was missing.

She didn't quite understand the way interest worked, and Phyllis was too afraid to ask at the counter in case they would embarrass her. She just let things lie and kept quiet.

It was one afternoon when Phyllis went to the Bank to withdraw some money only to be told by the cashier that the Bank Manager would like to see her. She wondered why she was to be seen by her Bank Manager and just thought it was their routine.

However the Bank Manager was very cross with her and told her that if she were to ever set foot in the Bank again; he would call the police and have her put into Jail.

So ashamed and embarrassed Phyllis was in tears. When she asked the manager why he told her not to pretend that she didn't know. But then somehow the manager took pity on her and realised she clearly did not know; she did not have one tiny clue of what was happening.

He brought her into the back and into his office and sat her down with some tissues.

It was there she discovered that Mr. Titus Roberts Junior and his sister in Law Matilda Roberts had been visiting the bank pretending to be Mr and Mrs Roberts and withdrawing her money.

Money from Phyllis's account had been taken out by them. The Bank Manager thought Phyllis was part of it as she came in to withdraw money. The manager could clearly see that she had nothing to do with it and suggested that she take legal steps towards him as this was fraud.

The Bank Manager was well within in his rights to call the police and have Junior and his sister in Law charged but he could see Phyllis's desperate and worried state and told her to open a new Bank account somewhere else and that if Junior were to ever put his foot back in this bank again then the police would be called.

Phyllis worried more now; does she tell him? Or let Junior carry on and go to the Bank knowing he will be arrested or leave things as they are? Either way Junior would be mad and Phyllis wasn't sure whether she would end up paying for it by being in the firing line.

So instead Phyllis told her brother in Law Gideon that she had to change banks as money had been taken out of her account. She knew Gideon would tell Junior this and he would not have the gall to ask her which bank.

PART SIXTEEN

- Pick your Poison-

Phyllis would struggle to find a decent Childminder who could look after her young daughter while she worked.

In those days no one would be registered; women would do it to earn money while they were able to stay at home.

Husbands were usually out working during the day, so it was a way to bring some extra money into the home. Plus by the time the husband got home from work the children were collected, house was tidy and dinner was on the table so there was nothing to disturb the home life of the man of the house. Except when children would be collected late!

Nothing worse than returning home after a hard days work only to find your home full of screaming children running around who were not even your own!!

The extra money that came into the home was often sent to the West Indies for the families.

It was quite normal for children to be raised by Grandparents who stayed in the West Indies.

Once the parents had settled here in the UK they would collect or have their children brought to England to be with the family again. It would sometimes take years to save money for the flight tickets; extra room for the new family member and depending on the age of the child; it would take quite some time for the children themselves to settle and adjust.

School would be tough being children of first generation immigrants. I often wondered why they were never called Ex- Pats. Name calling,

teasing, segregation, unkind teachers. Black children found it hard and some would rebel; few would try!

Parents would have difficulty understanding this and simply teach their children to be proud of their colour and to listen to the teacher. The parents never had any racial discrimination where they were from; there was no diversity; no colour difference apart from the shades so they had no words to strengthen the children with; plus where they were from, everyone would have the upmost respect for teachers and therefore the children were expected to be the same way to the teachers here.

It was equally hard for the child who came over to join the family in England. When the children came over there were usually additional siblings who they hadn't met and who were born while the older children were still in the West Indies. Being strangers to each other was difficult as the child from back home usually felt resentment for being left and then brought back to be with a larger family. One minute they would be left by their parents and were brought up by their Grandparents; only to leave them to come to cold England. Homesick was not the word and West Indians were very much Victorian in their ways. Children should be seen and not heard, hardly no affection given so there was no talking or reassuring the children who were sad and lonely and in a strange place with new siblings. They just had to get on with it and being teased for having an accent; these children had a lot to encounter from school and from home. So you can understand why a lot of them would have rebelled. They felt unloved and that they didn't belong anywhere; in no man's land but expected to just fit in with the click of the fingers.

Now because the children from back home knew how to cook, wash and clean, this is often what they would be doing around their home once they arrived in England. It was usual for the children born in England to be treated like royalty, while the ones from back home were like unpaid hired help. Not all families I must add. These usually were families who had daughters brought over and depending on their age as well would have many chores to do.

Some children were left as babies and as soon as they didn't need to be breastfed the parents would be off but some left at an older age.

Gifts and money was always sent back home and it was always such a treat to have clothes and items received from England.

Childminders were not reliable. Sometimes they would have far too many children in their care, babies and pre school age.

Phyllis would bring Andrea early in the morning depending on her shift. Yorkshire was so cold, especially in the mornings so Andrea would be wearing trousers to keep her little legs warm. At times the childminders would not even be up; let alone dressed and ready to mind the children.

Phyllis would bring food and treats for Andrea together with a change of clothes and a few instructions.

On collecting Andrea, Phyllis once noticed that Andrea would still be wearing the trousers from the morning. When asked, the minder would say that Andrea had an accident so had to change back into the trousers and that the dress had been washed.

This was happening far too often until Phyllis later found out that the woman was sending Andrea's clothes home to her own children in the West Indies. The food that was given to the minder for Andrea was being fed to her own children to save the child minder cooking. Poor Andrea was coming home terribly hungry.

So another child minder would be found which usually meant a chat outside the local post office or in the laundrette and a verbal agreement made with an address and directions given.

Childminders would agree to look after Andrea but not be there when she arrived in the morning; maybe it was too early for them or they just failed to answer the door. Nothing was in writing, no agreement or anything signed; everything was done verbally.

Childminders would have children while other people would visit the house for chats and gossip so not much attention was given to the children if any! There were times when Andrea would simply scream her head off when Phyllis handed Andrea over.

Phyllis would have to make up some excuse and not allow Andrea to stay there as she knew something had gone on. Poor Andrea; poor Phyllis it couldn't have been pleasant for either of them.

God bless the matron as she knew Phyllis was having it hard and would often allow her to bring Andrea to work, especially when she was on night duty. They would make up a little bed for Andrea in the nurses quarters. Phyllis and other nurses would check up on Andrea but there was no need; she was always fast asleep.

Junior would still be coming and going but his homecoming was less frequent. He wouldn't even leave any money for Phyllis; which was a blessing as that meant he would have no right to her or anything she purchased now that she had another mouth to feed. What Junior earned; Junior kept.

There were times when Phyllis and Andrea returned home and all the food that had been made for the evening meal for them would be eaten. Junior had been home and probably searched around for money and ate everything leaving nothing to eat.

Andrea's little hands would be so cold even with gloves on. Phyllis would have to turn on the oven for instant heat and boil the kettle to mix with cold water so that Andrea could put her little hands into the bowl to get them warm.

Nothing in the cupboards but flour and sugar and ingredients you couldn't make anything with. But this was Phyllis who had previously cooked for all and sundry and would know how to turn leftovers into a meal fit for a King.

Phyllis would open a tin of corned beef, cut up and fry onions and tomatoes into a pulp and make a corned beef hash. No rice but she would add water to flour, kneed it into flat round pieces and bake in the oven; there; a decent meal for two.

Junior was once there when Phyllis returned home from work. He would be sitting in the chair as if he'd been waiting all day long.

No doubt he had already searched the rooms and cupboards for money; but to no avail; not now that Phyllis had a new Bank Account.

Phyllis needed to get change for the gas meter so left Andrea with him while she went next door for some change.

When she got back Andrea had run to her and clung on to her tightly. When Phyllis picked her up she noticed that Andrea's dress which was cream, had green stains on the back and was wet.

Their couch was green and Phyllis realised that Andrea had wet herself through fear of this man. Too scared to even ask for the toilet let alone get up and go herself; Andrea had stayed seated on the coach and was petrified. Whether she actually needed to go or was just so scared of Junior; either way; she wet herself.

Phyllis took Andrea into the bathroom and cleaned and changed her daughter while they both cried, cried and cried.

Junior must have hard the cries because when Phyllis came out of the bathroom she had seen that Junior had taken all of the clothes he owned from the flat and left. Junior had left Phyllis and his young daughter but had also left them with unpaid bills and empty food cupboards.

Phyllis knew he had left; which was probably what he came back to say but due to the incident with Andrea wetting herself couldn't find it in his heart to tell her. Either that; or he just couldn't find his heart period.

So there was Phyllis with a young child and no husband; but still a sense of happiness and relief filled her knowing he would not be back again; or would he!

PART SEVENTEEN

-Denial is a River in Egypt-

There was Junior again up to his old tricks of simply turning up out of the blue and in the night purely to claim his conjugal rights. Phyllis would detest him even more. Not only for his action but also for the comment he would often make soon after. "You "can" go with other men you know; it doesn't have to be just me" and with that he would be gone into the dead of the night.

She would never understand his train of thought; even if she stayed with him for a million years!

Phyllis hated herself for not putting up any kind of resistance, she really did. That's when she would throw herself into work and looking after Andrea. Anything to take her mind off of those nights. She would become so angry thinking about it that she would occupy herself with work, reading the bible and praying really hard. Cooking and cleaning and looking after Andrea would become her new hobby. What else was there for her to do? But it was not Phyllis who needed to be forgiven!

Whilst collecting Andrea from a childminder one afternoon; one that seemed to have lasted for longer than two weeks, Phyllis felt pain to her lower groin area.

She thought it had been something she ate or even wind but it lasted far too long for either.

After a couple of days it had become worse and when she couldn't bare the pain any longer she went to the Doctors. In those days you could just arrive at the surgery and shout out "Who am I after?" and the last patient

would make some kind of reference to indicate they were last and so you would go in after them. A system that worked very well for many years.

Phyllis hoped and prayed hard that she wouldn't be pregnant again as the Doctor began to examine her.

A urine test was taken and antibiotics given for the pain and discomfort. She was told to return when the test results were back.

Strangely Phyllis received a telephone call from the Doctor during her shift and was told to visit the surgery as soon as she could.

She asked the Doctor If she were with child again. "We shall discuss this when you visit" was his firm reply.

Oh how this worried her even more, she left work before her shift ended and went straight to the surgery; she would collect Andrea later on as it was still early.

The Doctor sat her down and basically told her that she had caught an STD (sexual Transmitted Disease). Phyllis had no idea what that was and thought it were some kind of bug she had picked up from the hospital.

The Doctor asked how long she had been married and how things were at home and how was she coping with work and a young child. Still carrying on with the Victorian way of life; Phyllis said she was fine; hoping the Doctor wasn't able to read between the lines and tell she was hiding things.

The doctor moved his chair closer to her to explain exactly what an STD was and to tell her that her husband was having outside relationships. Phyllis still didn't quite get what she was being told so the Doctor broke it down clearly for her. "The disease you contracted was from your husband who has been sleeping with men."

Phyllis was in deep shock and stared at the Doctor with her mouth wide open as she flunked back onto the chair.

The Doctor advised Phyllis to take Junior to court and that he would support her by giving evidence against him.

Phyllis didn't understand a word of what she was being told, nothing made sense. It was all so surreal; which had left her in quite a daze.

She collected Andrea from the childminder and went home with more medication after visiting the local pharmacist. She was still in a complete daze and began questioning herself about Junior's actions and habits.

Phyllis didn't believe it and was in total denial. Why would he sleep with men? No way! She would not believe it. Out of all of the bad and wicked things there was about Junior he is not a homosexual. The Doctor has this completely wrong. Junior is married to me; he has a daughter, his family are raised in the Church, he was brought up fearing the word of God; his father was a minister in the local Church and greatly respected for goodness sake; how on earth can he be homosexual...

This is what Phyllis kept on telling herself; this is what she believed.

She carried on with work and reading her Bible and praying and looking after her daughter but refused to believe the doctors diagnoses.

She had to go back to the Doctor to receive the all clear from him and again the Doctor asked if she had thought any more about taking her husband to court.

She said No; she hadn't thought about it and neither would she do it.

The Doctor asked where her husband was and when she had last seen him.

Phyllis felt embarrassed as she could not give him an answer.

That's when the penny dropped; where was Junior? Where was he staying? And more to the point; who was he staying with?

Not only had Junior left his wife and young daughter; he had also left unpaid bills behind.

Phyllis had visits from the Coal man and the electric company who threatened to switch off her utilities. All she could do was tell them that her husband had left her and she will try to make the payments as often as she could.

Phyllis was struggling now, her pay would have to stretch its furthest in order to make ends meet.

She could no longer send money home to her mother to help her even though Harriet was probably struggling a lot more.

When West Indian women would see Phyllis looking sad and tired they suggested to send Andrea home to be with her Grandparents.

"Not while I am living and breathing. She is my child" was her reply. How could she even think of being without her dear beautiful daughter? And more to the point; who would she stay with in the West Indies anyway. Her own mother couldn't look after Phyllis so how could she send her child there? No way; not in this life time.

PART EIGHTEEN

-A Helping Hand-

When it were possible Phyllis would also send money to Junior's mother as well as her own. But not now; not when she was struggling with having to juggle and make sacrifices in her own life.

But prior to the juggling Phyllis had managed to send a couple of pounds over. Air-Mail took so long to get across in those days and what with some folk being illiterate by the time they would receive letters and find someone to read it and write the reply and get to the post office and for the letter to travel; it would be months before you received a response.

It wasn't necessary to wait for a reply; if you had something to say or send; it would be done regardless.

Phyllis received a letter from Junior's mother soon after she had sent some money. She thought it was a quick reply but little did she know, her letter had not yet arrived with Junior's mother.

The letter she received from his mother was awful; telling Phyllis that she is a terrible woman and wife to her son, saying how dare she treat her son so badly; that she had all kinds of men bringing her home and not leaving until the early hours of the morning; and how Phyllis should rot in hell.

Phyllis was very upset with the letter and even more frustrated with herself for sending the money, but she wasn't to know.

It became clear that Junior had secretly written to his mother about Phyllis; all bad and untruths of course! That was the last time Phyllis would send her as much as a dime.

Then on the other side of the coin there was news from Phyllis's cousin Teacher Sally saying that when she sent money and gifts to her mother, Phyllis's other sisters would take it from her and only visit when money and gifts were received.

Poor Phyllis; money was getting sent to the wrong person on both counts; but it wasn't long before Phyllis received a letter from her Mother-in-law thanking her for the money and how it came in handy and what a good daughter-in- law she was etc etc etc; that letter was never read again.

A hospital porter by the name of Michael Clarkson would often try to speak to Phyllis but she wasn't interested. The odd hello was fine just to be polite but nothing else.

Michael would see her at the bus stop at times and offer to drive her home.

Phyllis often declined until one evening on a dark cold and rainy night Phyllis thought it wise to accept. He drove her to the childminder to collect Andrea and then to her door, made sure they both went in safe and drove off. This became more frequent in a subtle kind of way to the point where Phyllis actually looked out for him at the bus stop. Finally she was one of the nurses who would enjoy being collected and driven home.

Although Michael was only a janitor at the hospital he could fix anything he put his hands on; literally! Electric, wood, water; he reminded Phyllis of her own Grandfather who would be good at making all kinds of things with his hands.

Michael was good looking with sideburns and was always dressed neatly; even under his overalls he would be wearing a shirt and tie.

Michael would help Phyllis carry her shopping to the door; he would give her money towards the electric and coal bills to avoid being cut off.

It was very hard for her to accept but she knew it was the best thing.

How could she thank this man? he was so kind and thoughtful and didn't ask for a single penny in return. He would say he didn't like to see anyone suffer and if he can help; he will.

He was a gentleman, he would bring shopping for Phyllis with some treats for Andrea. But Andrea was cautious of any man and stayed close to her mum. He didn't even stay over; he would visit and help with odd jobs that needed to be done, say good night and leave.

But news travels fast doesn't it, especially in small communities. Junior turned up, in the night, completely out of the blue.

Obviously hoping to catch Phyllis in bed with this man he had heard was "visiting". But as no one was in the marital bed he snuck in. Phyllis tried to fight him off as much as she could. But Junior was far too strong for her little frail body. Junior won and although delighted that the rumours were probably wrong was pleased that he could claim his conjugal rights even if it were by force and so what if it meant him leaving soon after; again..

He didn't even look in on his daughter!

Oh how Phyllis wished she could hate that man: but being a woman raised in the Church she could only detest his ways. She detested everything about him, how he ate his food with the veins on his temple pulsating, how he would always be so immaculately dressed; how he would refuse to interact with his daughter; how he would take her money and eat their food and come and go and lie and cheat oh how she detested him.

Michael met her from work one evening soon after Junior's last visit.

She collected Andrea from the childminders and cooked a nice meal for the three of them. It was lovely to see Andrea hand him one of her toys; which was obviously the seal of approval to her.

Pity it couldn't be the same with her own Father; No, it was not a pity actually..

Phyllis bathed her daughter and put her to bed. When she came out she saw Michael washing dishes, she joined him but took over as Phyllis wasn't used to this. But it was nothing to Michael in fact this was quite normal to him.

They tidied up the kitchen and chatted together (another rare moment) She told Michael about Junior; not everything of course, and certainly not the recent events or conclusions to his lifestyle.

It was such a nice evening and one thing led to another; but Phyllis didn't mind this (anything to block out Junior's previous behaviour) she didn't mind this kind of attention, this kind of loving, this kind of attentiveness; this she didn't mind at all.

PART NINETEEN

Lies, Lies and more Lies!!

It was very unusual for Phyllis's brother -in-law to visit her; so you can imagine her surprise when she arrived home one evening to find Gideon waiting for her on the front steps.

Just as well it was only her and Andrea returning home on this occasion!

They greeted one another on the steps and Gideon tickled Andrea under her chin; but Andrea was still weary of men even though he were her Uncle, she backed away from his hand and hid behind Phyllis. He had no chance!

She invited Gideon inside while she wondered to herself why he had visited. Phyllis offered and made him a cup of tea and politely asked how he had been.

They had got on relatively well in the past until the episode with the bank and his wife impersonating and stealing her money. Funny how nothing was said about that. Gideon never asked to hear her side or apologise for his wife's behaviour.

Still; he's here now and maybe he's come for that reason. Late; but still, his conscience is finally pricking him.

Well; that's what Phyllis thought he was there for; what else? Surely if anything had happened to Junior; she as his wife would have been informed first. Gideon sat down very formally at the table not on the sofa, removing his hat and drinking tea from the cup whilst holding the saucer.

Phyllis could hold on no longer "Was there something in particular that you wanted Gideon?"

He shifted uncomfortably while he crossed over his other leg.

"There are rumours going around that you are inviting and coming home with different men all the time"

Phyllis was not expecting that and was very shocked at his accusations. She asked who had told him such a thing. He did not answer. Instead he went on and accused her of throwing Junior out of the home and telling her that it was wrong for her to prevent him from seeing his daughter.

Phyllis gave a nervous laugh as she was so flabbergasted with this made up rumour.

Gideon said she was disgusting and only pretended to carry herself like a lady when she was nothing but a back street whore.

Well that was it; Phyllis was not going to allow him to disrespect her with such lies in her own home and in front of her daughter.

She told him to get out; to leave and never to speak like that to her again. Gideon became angry and asked how she could behave that way to his brother; after all he had done for her. Paying her fares to come to England; making sure she had a home; marrying her; encouraging her to become a nurse.

Phyllis could only see red at this time and had to open her mouth and let out some home truths to him.

"For your information Mr Roberts; Mr. Gideon Roberts your dear brother did not pay my fare to come to England. My Uncle paid it." Gideon's face showed nothing but embarrassment but was still confused. This had not been what his brother had told him. "Your brother has caused me nothing but heart ache and pain; your brother who refuses to put a single penny from his so called hard earned wages on the table for his family. Your dear brother who does nothing but search and take money from me which has been hidden from him in the first place; your dear brother who cooks food and hides it under lock and key in the wardrobe where I have to come home and cook for me and his daughter."

Gideon's mouth was wide open not sure whether to speak up or stay quiet; he chose the latter!

"And can I add at this point that your dear brother did not help neither encourage me in the slightest to obtain the job as a nurse; he wanted me to work in a factory with the rest of his dead beat family. The wedding dress was borrowed, I was not allowed to invite any of my family to my

own wedding. It was your dear wife and brother who went to the bank where your wife pretended to be me so they could take "my" hard earned money from "my" bank account. So when you decide to come into my home Gideon with the lies your brother has fed you with; seek for the truth first. And don't get me started on your dear wife!"

Phyllis sat down with exhaustion. She had shocked herself by saying all she had. Maybe she had said too much but she could never let the Roberts family blame her for Junior's wrong doing.

Gideon was adamant that Phyllis was lying to save the embarrassment of having another man around in their home and still accused her of lying. "My brother would never do such a thing. We all grew up back home as a family. I know my brother. He would never treat his wife and child in that way; never. Why would you lie. Junior was right you are a lying whore"

Andrea would be crying with the raised voices and feeling very upset. She could only put this down to all men coming to upset her mother.

"I suppose your brother told you that he sleeps with men did he; that he gave me a sexually transmitted disease. I suppose he told you that Gideon? that he comes and goes as he pleases. That I never see him from one day to the next. That he's left me with unpaid bills where I have men knocking on the door for their money: I suppose your dear brother told you all of that did he?"

One minute Gideon was on his feet ready to leave but hearing that from her he quickly sat down as though he were about to faint. He sat straight down with his eyes wide open unable to believe what had just been said. Gideon did not say a single word; he couldn't; words failed to leave his mouth.

He used the table to help steady himself to his feet; placed his hat on his head and left.

Phyllis heard the door close with a silent clunk and then slow footsteps down the stairs to the main front door; again with a silent clunk.

Phyllis was shaking; her hands trembled as she picked up the cup and saucer and carried them to the kitchen: she too was in shock.

Never had she had to raise her voice and speak to anyone in those tones. But she felt good: it's just a pity it was to the wrong person.

She was worried now. Worried in case Gideon went back and told Junior; as up until that day Phyllis had never let on to Junior that she had

been under medical care with the tablets and the blood test and finding out from the Doctor that she had caught a sexually transmitted disease from her husband. Junior would be as mad as hell when he knew and would come flying through the door at any given moment. That scared her more than anything.

PART TWENTY

One way ticket for two

Phyllis couldn't settle in her own home after the confrontation she recently had with Gideon. She was so worried that Junior would arrive in the dead of night and continue with his unpleasant ways. He had every reason to turn up especially now with the news from his brother.

It seemed that the rumours trailed out to the corner shops, the Local Post Office and even the laundrette as everywhere Phyllis went she felt that she was being talked and whispered about.

At the bus stop on her way to work one afternoon she was certain she heard two young women say "That's her; the one who's husband goes with men!". She went cold inside, she couldn't swallow, it felt as though she had a big ball stuck in her throat. She tried to act as though it wasn't her; but they knew it was her and Phyllis also knew they were right.

How could something like that get out? Who else would have known? Who would have been so bitter to tell anyone?

This is a family matter and was far too personal to become local gossip. Phyllis felt physically sick inside. This was a big matter which left her feeling that it would be best if she just walked away fast and kept her head down.

This deep dark secret did not want to go away; whispers were being heard in the staff room at work as well as the bus stop and outside the hospital gates. This was becoming very embarrassing for her.

One evening whilst on duty she decided to take a walk within the grounds to look for Michael, her current companion. She needed to talk to someone as this was beginning to choke her.

She saw his car in the car park grounds so she knew he was at work, but being on duty she needed to get back onto the ward; she'd look for him another time. Strange that he hadn't come looking for her though.

Phyllis started to feel slightly queasy in the evenings. She remembered when she last felt this way, when she was working in the theatre. The smell of the blood made her feel faint however she couldn't work out why she was feeling this way again. Maybe it will pass.

A couple of days had passed and the rumours had spilt to the childminder who looked after Andrea.

The lady said that she had heard rumours that Andrea's father was going with men and other mothers were refusing to bring their children and babies there if Andrea still attended.

This was getting too much for her now; it seemed everywhere she turned people were talking. Something had to be done; but what?

She found another childminder for Andrea; probably the only one left in Yorkshire that she hadn't tried!

Still feeling queasy through most of the day Phyllis decided to stop by at the Doctors to find out what this sick feeling was all about.

Just as she was about to be called in to the Doctor it hit her like a ton of bricks; "I bet I'm pregnant!".

No need for the Doctor to confirm anything now, she knew it straight away but as she was there she sat down and told the Doctor all that had been going on.

The Doctor asked if she wanted to go ahead with the pregnancy and that it wasn't too late for a termination; in fact now would be a good time before she started to show. Plus with all of the rumours and all, things would get too much for her and she may just end up losing it so it would probably be best to terminate it medically rather than to miscarry.

Phyllis was totally against this and thanked the Doctor before she left.

She shut the door and stood with her back and head against it, worrying about her next chapter. For a split second she took on board what the Dr had said. A split second passed and Phyllis gained strength; straightened

her back, came away from the door, put her best foot forward and off she went with her head held high.

This was serious and getting too much for her as she was still on Red Alert waiting for Junior to show up at any minute.

Alone and pregnant; then it suddenly dawned on her "Who is the father?"

Phyllis carried on with work regardless of her situation. How she managed it all was anyone's guess!

She saw Michael in the corridor from afar. She wasn't in the mood for pleasantries but wondered why he hadn't been around.

She waited for him to come down from the ladder and asked if he was ok and why he was keeping his distance. He looked embarrassed and Phyllis just assumed that he was interested in another nurse; it happens. But then he told her that he had heard rumours. "Which rumours?" She asked.

"Rumours that your husband is looking for me." He answered matter of factly.

Phyllis was quite relieved as she thought they were rumours that Junior's sexuality had got this far; but they were probably next.

"I cannot afford any trouble, I need to work I need this job. I have a family back home in Jamaica to look after"

Phyllis was shocked to hear this. "You mean you have a family back home and you play around with me? Is that it? You take me for some kind of a loose woman who carries on this way? Is that it?"

"No. Not a loose woman at all; But Phyllis you too are married! I was happy to help you. I knew you were in a mess and offered what I could to help. We were two lonely people Phyllis; two lonely people who happened to be married!"

She knew that what he was saying were true; she just wished he had been man enough to tell her at the beginning..

"This is not the place for this kind of discussion; let me visit you tonight so we can talk?" Michael had suggested.

"Huh; but aren't you scared? my husband is looking for you remember!" And with that she spun on her heals and headed for the ward.

Phyllis couldn't keep her mind on her job whilst on duty, she was miles away thinking about all kinds of plans and decisions.

She knew she couldn't stand the chit chat wherever she went; people pointing the finger at her from across the street, no family of her own, or any of Junior's family on her side, pregnant and not knowing who the father is; her homosexual husband or the married hospital janitor; oh Lord, pick your poison!!

She knew she had to get away; that was for sure.

When she had the chance she rang her cousin in Acton, Liz and told her all what was going on.

"Just come to London, stay with me I'll look after you all." Was her comforting response.

A huge sigh of relief came with floods of tears in the telephone box.

Phyllis headed for the Matron's office the very next day and told her that she had to leave; she told the Matron that her mother was not well and therefore had to go back to the West Indies to look after her.

She hated lying but she had no choice. How could she divulge such personal matters. The Matron was in tears as she really liked Phyllis but knew she couldn't say anything that would make her change her mind. She told Phyllis that if she should ever wish to return, there's always a job here for her.

Phyllis left her office in tears after hugging the Matron and with leaving she bumped into Michael. She told him she was leaving the hospital. She didn't say where she was going, just that she were leaving and he didn't ask where she was going.

"It's a shame things didn't work" he said.

"Yes, it's a shame you were not honest Michael and I see that my husband has not found you, but like you said; they were rumours"

"Goodbye Michael and thank you for your help"

Again she spun on her heels without waiting for any reply.

Next stop would soon be to the train station to purchase one adult and one child ticket to Paddington London "One Way Please, No Return!" Phyllis could not wait to say that very sentence.

PART TWENTY ONE

This Time is Right..

So that was it; her mind was made up. Her, her daughter and her unborn child were leaving Yorkshire for London.

She had already told Matron so that was sorted. Now there was no one else to tell apart from the girls at work. Oh but second thoughts, gossip would start up again; that's if they ever died down in the first place.

Phyllis had told Matron she was going back to the West Indies to look after her sick Mother so how could she tell other nurses that she was going to London to get away from her awful husband? That would be so wrong; No; she'll leave things as they were; who cared anyway?

As she had to give two weeks notice at work; she decided to leave at the end of that third week. She wanted to make sure everything was sorted before she left; a bit difficult to do while she was still working. So much to do with so little time.

Phyllis spoke to her cousin again to make sure all was still ok before she purchased the ticket. This was a big step so she had to be sure.

All was well, she would eventually stay in South Hall with her brother Oscar after spending a couple of weeks with Liz. Oscar had a big house and rented out rooms. His wife Marie was also in nursing so already Phyllis had something in common with a family member.

Phyllis was really looking forward to a change, a good change, an easy life without having to keep looking over her shoulder when she was out and worrying that Junior would turn up when she was at home. Oh how she longed for this easy life.

She started packing bit by bit each evening; washing and ironing clothes to be packed. She had her one battered suit case that she bought from the West Indies but she would need a much bigger one for the two of them / three!!

Being pregnant wasn't always on the forefront of her mind until she felt that queasy feeling again. She had too much to do to be planning for the arrival of her second born; but once things were settled and she were more focused; further planning would commence.

But Phyllis was getting tired with being pregnant; working; tending to her daughter and getting ready for the big move. She needed rest; but she also needed to get things moving.

Leaving for work one morning she had most things packed up and ready to be boxed up. Sheets ironed and stacked on the end of the bed for packing, clothes neatly folded on the seat of the chair as well as the two arms. Cutlery; pots and pans with crockery were sitting on the table waiting to be placed into boxes for the move. She would collect some boxes on her way home to put them in. The time was drawing near; excitement or trepidation? A mixture of both I think; fear of the Unknown.

Phyllis was on split duty that day and came home at lunch time with a few boxes but as she walked through the door, she had a strong feeling Junior was around; she could smell his scent. Her stomach was in knots as she didn't know if he were inside the flat somewhere waiting for her. Fear found her before anything else. She looked in all the rooms but he wasn't there. This made her even more frightened; in case he came back or if he was hiding somewhere and about to jump out. Although he didn't jump out from anywhere; Phyllis thought the place looked a bit strange; just not how she left it was when she left for work.

She knew Junior had been there; that was it; he had taken things. The sheets were no longer on the bed; nowhere else to be honest. The clothes had been shuffled and moved. Some had been moved from the arm of the chair and you could tell some had been ruffled on the seat. What did he want? She thought..

She looked all around the two bedroom flat only to see that Junior had taken almost everything. All the things that Phyllis had packed up ready to be boxed; Junior had taken them.

Almost everything was gone, but he had left some spoons, the iron with the ironing board and the wedding ring, all on the table.

He was so intimidating and such a bully; the wedding ring that was left was hers. She kept it in her drawer next to her bed in the same drawer as her Bible. Junior had been busy and up to his old tricks searching again, found the ring and placed it on the table so Phyllis could see what he had done.

She was so upset; she had everything sorted; but yet again Junior had to come along and spoil things. Good thing she had not bought the tickets and left them lying around as that would have given everything away.

Phyllis had to leave after lunch to get back to work to start the other half of her duty.

As she was going downstairs one of the girls from the flat below had stopped her.

"That husband of yours is no good Phyllis; has he gone now?" She asked. Phyllis was embarrassed as she knew they heard everything that was going on from down there.

"Yes he's gone"

"Well I am pleased; you'll manage without him you'll see. I've seen him many times going into work in the factory. A man waits for him outside and your husband gives him money. What's that money for Phyllis? Who is that man? They're not related because he's a white man? Do you know him; tall man with a small beard; always wears a hat and a long grey rain coat"

Phyllis was shocked but tried not to show it. "No, I don't know who it is. I must go. I am due on the ward shortly"

"Oh of course; you do a great job you nurses do"

And with that Phyllis was off to work where she decided to buy her ticket for the next week as soon as she finished at the hospital. Why hang around!!

But how dare he come in and clear the marital home of everything Phyllis had purchased? And who was this man Junior gave money to?

To be honest; she didn't really care. In all honesty she was glad of the fact that she had argued with Gideon and just fortunate that Junior hadn't come to her all guns a blazing. Which could only mean one thing; Gideon hadn't told Junior. Could Gideon have known all along? And now it has

been confirmed that he is giving his money to someone confirms all that the Doctor had told her.

Even though she knew the Doctor must have been right; there was always an element of doubt at the back of her mind. All things have come together now which confirms it all.

Oh there were so many reasons for Phyllis to get out and leave this cold and lonely town behind; so many reasons. She felt as though she had no place there. She had never felt settled; but to be honest: when had she ever had that feeling of contentment? Only at times in St. Lucia; never in Dennery and certainly never in Yorkshire. Yes; time for her to leave this cold and lonely town and head for London where she at least will have her family for solace. Time to move To Pastures New...

I dedicate the first book of the trilogy sequel Labour of Love to my dear friend Penny who planted the seed for this book when she was diagnosed with cancer. She had asked for a list of good books that I had read but I said I would do better; I decided to send her chapters of my life. But I couldn't start with me; I had to come from somewhere and so did my mother and so did her mother and so the book began. As I completed each chapter I sent them to her to read while she convalesced. My sister would also receive a chapter where she would reply with corrections; my sister; my rock and my role model for helping with the research and for her memory which assisted in many chapters.

I also dedicate this book to my dear son, for him to understand how important it is to follow his passion.

Lightning Source UK Ltd.
Milton Keynes UK
UKOW02f0251090716

277977UK00001B/17/P